# Lyrics Of Mature Hearts
### Edited by Bob McNeil

**ALSO BY GORDON P. BOIS**

**Poetry**

The Revolving Door

Multiplicity

What I See Is What You Get

Another Kick At The Can

THE 5TH

What He Said.

THE WASHBOARD EFFECT

MURDERING THE THIRD

Kit & Caboodle

Leaping Over Landmines

**Quotes**

WEATHERING STONE

ON WRITING

# Introduction
## by Bob McNeil

Let's face it, the media, which thrives on exploiting insecurities, believes in ageism. Unquestionably, judging by the numerous advertisements for ways to reverse the aging process, it despises older people. Each product says it's a time machine for removing crow's feet, marionette lines, or turkey necks. Rest be assured, if these commercials could come up with canvases for selling souls, a lot of senior citizens and middle-aged individuals would wind up like Dorian Gray.

Nonetheless, to me, white follicles and wrinkles are medals. Awarded for longtime service, they indicate that I survived battles with my body and the world beyond. Sure, life's later years are difficult. But, compared with earlier stages, the aging process is noble.

Upon starting this anthology endeavor, I searched for poets, who like me, did not cling to youth the way hairspray holds a combover. Honestly, at the very beginning, many contributors avoided the subject as if they were bats fleeing the dawn. Others, thankfully, confronted the severe light of what old age means. Their verses are replete with candor, not candy.

So, out of gratitude for those honest poets, in the manner of numerous introductions for anthologies, I could have enumerated certain verses or lines from this compilation expounding upon the points made thus far. However, considering that the printed work is in your hands, what would be the point? Because the collection bears the names of the publisher and the editor, it is clear that we are proud. The reason for our admiration is simple. Resulting from experiences, knowledge, and artistry, these poets express the myriad detestable and delightful aspects of adulthood. These writers are the embodiment of this Betty Friedan quote: "Aging is not lost youth but a new stage of opportunity and strength."

# Lyrics Of Mature Hearts
### Edited by Bob McNeil

Espanola, Ontario
Canada

**Lyrics Of Mature Hearts**
**A Poetry Anthology**

Copyright © 2019 Lyrics of Mature Hearts – by Gordon P. Bois.

Contributing Editors: Bob McNeil and Gordon P. Bois

Cover Illustration: George Juan Vivo.

File Set-up: Gordon P. Bois

Additional File Set-up/Cover Revisions: William J. Leeney

Gordon Bois Publications' books can be ordered at www.gordonsbookshelf.com and www.amazon.com.

All rights reserved by individual contributors relevant to their contributions.
No part of this publication may be reproduced, distributed, or transmitted in any form or by any means, including photocopying, recording, or other electronic or mechanical methods, without written permission from the publisher, except in the case of brief quotations embodied in critical articles, studies, reviews and certain other non-commercial uses permitted by copyright law. For permission requests, email the publisher via the web address below.

Gordon Bois Publications,
Espanola, Ontario
www.gordonsbookshelf.com

# Contents

## My Relationship With Time
Every Man Has His Price by Will Mayo .................................................5
My Body and Me by John Maney ..........................................................6
Tomorrow Is Easy, but Today Is Uncharted by Jonathan Yungkans..................7
Lichen by Kevin Miller ........................................................................8
Now I'm Sixty-Two by James Walton ....................................................9
Regret by Edna Garcia........................................................................10
A Look of Glass Stops You by Jonathan Yungkans ...............................11
The Crippled Spectacle by Lydia Percy ................................................13
Notes on Being Invisible by Silvia Blumenfeld......................................14
Flight by Linda Imbler........................................................................15
My Relationship with Time by Edward Thomas Dillon..........................16

## Grizzled Grace
Love does not end by Carmen E. Arroyo...............................................19
NEW AUTUMN LOVE by Claire Joysmith ..........................................21
35th Anniversary by Cynthia Pratt .......................................................22
House of Silence by C. Liegh McInnis .................................................23
Love's Equation by Joan McNerney .....................................................25
To A Lady by Robert Dickerson...........................................................26
Late-life Love by Kathy Lundy Derengowski .......................................27
Profound Love by Edna Garcia............................................................28
Archived by Bob McNeil ....................................................................29
GRIZZLED GRACE by Susan McMillan .............................................30
The Old Lovers by Kit Rohrbach.........................................................31
The Sum of Maturity's Rhythm by Bob McNeil ...................................32

## Just Hold Me
waiting for magic by Fred Simpson......................................................35
Untitled by E. Penniman James ...........................................................36
Just hold me by Jean Parrish................................................................37
Dirty Old Lady by Leslie Mills............................................................38

## Your Body Deserts You
Your Body Deserts You by Edward Thomas Dillon ...............................41
Rearview Mirror by Karla Linn Merrifield............................................42
The Caretaker by Karla Linn Merrifield ...............................................44

## Me And My Burden Of Bones
Embraceable You by Edward Thomas Dillon .......................................47
Her Candle by Carl Palmer .................................................................51
Me and My Burden of Bones by Will Mayo .........................................53
Between The Pages Of A Life by Will Mayo ........................................54

Notes on the Poets ..............................................................................55
About The Publisher ...........................................................................59

# Lyrics Of Mature Hearts

# My Relationship With Time

"Old age, believe me, is a good and pleasant thing. It is true you are gently shouldered off the stage, but then you are given such a comfortable front stall as spectator." -- Confucius

**Every Man Has His Price**

I think of countless friends and relatives
gone gray and dead with decay.
What a terrible price for this life!
And yet - and yet - there is beauty
that remains in the still and the dark
of one man's life passing by
To have, to strive, to love even.
And then to give it all up
for the goodness of time.
Surely worth every gray hair
and the beating of one dying heart.

by Will Mayo

**My Body and Me**

We have been together,
brown skin, muscle, bone,
breath, and blood
for a long time now.

You propelled me
up mountains and down
to the bottom of clear lakes
 where fish swam
in bodies different from ours
in places we could not stay.

You have taken me
places I dreamt of
and places of pain
I never want to revisit.
Through it all, you taught me
every breath.
Every moment, you taught me,
though I wasn't always listening.

When I was younger,
I wished we were taller.
When I got older,
I wished us thinner.

Sometimes I wished
we were faster.
Other times, I longed for sleep
that you would not give.

This morning, I woke
before sunrise to pray.
You lifted me from my bed
then brought me to my knees.

I closed my eyes.
When I opened them, I saw
the sunrise caress us.

You let me experience this.
You told me that "love
was all around us:
short,
fat,
just as we are."

by John Maney

**Tomorrow Is Easy, but Today Is Uncharted**
**(after John Ashbery)**

The fig tree has been denuding for the winter, an unhurried striptease,
a leaf or two at a time, soundless, as through the neck of an hourglass.

Even with a bright sun, I feel the cold as though my walls are glass.
I try not to think of sand—or my wits running out, for that matter.

I eye the summer discards, Decembered to stillness on St. Augustine,
salacious in their gentle beguilement of time, their lull into abeyance.

Quiet hides a dot-dash cloud of finches that races through my head;
they dart, scarcely tap midair as they flash and judder commotion.

Foliage curls, yellowed hands lepoarded with brown age spots.
Palms, upturned, bead fog that sweated off the sky hours ago.

I look at the back of my hand; its blotches, creased map of fullness,
diagram of place that isn't a place but still physical, a state of detritus.

Leaves, swept into their private landscape, remain intact, earthbound;
they persevere as they desiccate, crack like overheated stoneware,

like those stained, lengthening fissures that have aged into my brain:
fractured clay beneath a glazed shimmer held together as best it can.

by Jonathan Yungkans

**Lichen**

Alder trunks blossom
in hammered shield lichen.
Thin paper ears cupped
for western wren,
for the deer in the under-
story, the echo of sea lions
from the bay, for our foot-
fall mornings as we walk
our remaining years.
No one's counting days,
we count political years,
wish for rapid-time
to erase this election
even if it calls us closer
to kids coming for the keys,
suggesting smaller options,
fewer chores, someone
to help with the meds.
We laugh at Methuselah
Lichen. Our green ends frizzle.

by Kevin Miller

**Now I'm Sixty-Two**

I am fifteen years away

from the age my father reached

standing in the shade

of a forty-year-old apple tree

on an early autumn day,

with still no sign of rain,

and the ground that has cracked

like sore lips after oranges.

For decades, I've resisted

those crossed arms in an aging pout,

but it's only fair to tell you

that I've messed it up again.

A stranger to myself

more than a little bewildered

rolling among leaves of words I could never find

when it mattered to others,

that simple declaration out of inhibition

might have proved it all,

a theory of consequences

where love is animate of itself.

Out of this horrible day in a horrible season,

I'm collecting the genuine events

making ready a pelagic seedbed,

trying again for a new season's merciful shift.

by James Walton

**Regret**

Autumn came suddenly
Like a thief
Stealing my dreams
Of a youthful spring
Filled with new sunrises
Reviving my senses.

Autumn came suddenly
In the manner of a deceiver.
It made me confuse fleeting moments
Of success with unquestionable happiness.

Autumn came suddenly,
And with it, memories of vain,
Useless laurels
That I would gladly exchange
For some measure of happiness.

by Edna Garcia

**A Look of Glass Stops You**
**(after John Ashbery)**

Do I see myself? There is my excuse for breathing—
green eyes, red hair too soon since my last haircut

to regrow grey, though my balding pate scatters
stray hints that my bones ache non-arthritic sadness,

making autonomic respiration a curse. My fingers
mistype "bot" for "but." They're telling the truth—

waking is nothing I'd choose to do—just like typing
"misstyle" for "mistype" that somehow my presence

is an act of style. Change the hue. Watch your language.
Put on a Zoloft face. Green gets a wicked rap for envy—

manicured lawns and trees grow in narcissistic fervor—
and here I count devils in my details—totaling stones

that show in a crystalline river. The mirror is water,
doesn't wash clean, drowns if it inhales before it.

⁕


A Fireball bottle's sharp remains to grin from the street,
its label's dancing devil fresh blood or Mercurochrome
in hypomanic brightness. I kick label and glass to curb,

sweep its fragments of daylight from incoming cars—
the excuse of consideration to mask when, in the mirror,
I see the Fireball demon stare back, seeing which scab

in conscience is worth a pull this morning. Sun flashes
on the glass while blood oozes through wrinkles in a face
I'd never seen as me for the life of me, clear and void.

⁕


A mirror is glass and silver and laminated lies. A mirror
is where my self-esteem slides into the sink, is washed

into a purification or cleanliness that drains old skin, soap
and the scum some call my awkward questions, attempts

to break a clear hard surface into which I was born, walled,
from which I watch them spray polish my face, walk away.

⁕

11

Overripe figs become eyes. Pupils stare down terrain. Bees
wander in and out of vision, into pulp turned aqueous humor.
Widening perception, they hollow fruit into a hanging skin.
Eyes become their own mirrors, reflect choleric genomes
that bloomed. A Fireball label lies kicked amid grape leaves.

.

The fig tree at my door watches me. Neighboring bees,
like my own neighbors, buzz and collect as they observe.
My eyes take in their faces, reflections from their eyes
which hollow me from their apprehension and terror—
not what they see, but the overripe harvest they carry.
For bees and neighbors, it's in the guise of making honey,

but with sour nectar that sours hive, street, gaze above
my bathroom sink. I feel, razor-sharp as I try to shave,
a long glass fragment pasted to a prancing Fireball devil.

.

When I look into the mirror, I see. When I look into the mirror,
I see a truce between my life and my death, eyes that recede

toward a yellow fabric living-room chair, fresh mug of coffee,
ticking minutes, clock hands that refuse to budge. When I look

into the mirror, I see faces where the numbers on the clock dial
should smile, and in the glower of glass, I wish for a window

in hope of clearness that I am not, all streaked and scratched,
framed in chipping paint on wood. When I look into the mirror,

I make it a point to keep my glances short; one shot is enough
to sing and sting me into an oldies playlist of regrets for a day.

by Jonathan Yungkans

**The Crippled Spectacle**

Don't let me linger
somewhere in my own matter
be a sore to my eye
if I have grown slightly dimwitted
or visually dilapidated
crippled by time
don't hold me a patient in asylum
to be figured out like *Titicut Follies*
allow beg
me some
dignity
if the forward years are unkind
scaring one with cruelty
then allow death to sit upon my step
may petition the world to be hurled
out of the rotten bowels of society
to be remembered a muse.

by Lydia Percy

**Notes on Being Invisible**

We friends met for dinner, not too long ago,
and Helen said that she just didn't know.
We pondered together about when it had happened
over goblets of red. Now our spirits were dampened.

Then, Nancy remembered that she'd been fifty-three.
It was then she had finally, though strangely, felt free.
No longer obsessed with those thoughts of escaping
when quite suddenly it seemed, men had stopped gaping.

Oh, the clothes and that hair, the face and those curves,
that perfect small body and whom it serves,
the cruel, the relentless, and the constant critique
produced young women so obsequious and meek.

So, now we're old, and ironically, it's great
because now we come first and we don't ever wait.
We talk and laugh loudly, eat well and drink,
and most unequivocally, we always say what we think.

by Silvia Blumenfeld

**Flight**

I think of myself
as a bird with twigs to save,
for a nest of memories,
for remembrance of labors well done,
and much sweet music played.

I have, at times, been queen of all music,
enjoyed the zoom, the sweep, and the rush
of a soft landing after a rough flight.
I never found time for mocking the fates
at the fading view of the day
but made time, instead,
for singing life in deep-throated tones.

With dearest friends, there was never an end
to what we could talk about and learn,
no terminus to listing ways
in which we could leave the world a better place.
So we stayed patient and waited.
We marveled at how quickly time had elapsed
since the last sunset rolled along.
We hypothesized what might erase all our worlds,
and prognosticated when peace would come again.

I'll recall,
when my final dawn sneaks forward,
the many grades and pitfalls
I stumbled through while remaining upright.
I'll keep walking in shades of beauty,
seeing the twinkling stars play,
fold my frail wings in supplication,
and never cease to pray.
I'll survive the stormy blasts
to walk beneath the archway of a rainbow,
delighting that I did not fail.
And get there just in time to the wind-kissed sea,
then fly lightly on my way,
as the dim of my eyes arrives.

by Linda Imbler

**My Relationship with Time**

I'm renouncing my relationship with time.

We're done, we're through, it's over.

Though I've tried time and again

to reach time,

time has just ignored my calls

and gone her merry way.

Through many nights of insomnia,

time just lay there listless,

not even moving.

Then, in rare moments of rapturous joy,

time just flitted them all away,

spending my happiness

like a credit card diva gone amok.

Time got older and heavier

even gravity seemed to affect her.

Then, as I got older, she got meaner

and seemed to disappear every other day.

I file this brief with you, your honor,

I just want to make time go away

quickly.

by Edward Thomas Dillon

# Grizzled Grace

"Age does not protect you from love. But love, to some extent, protects you from age." -- Anaïs Nin

**Love does not end**

At my age, rest has come.
I know the silence of the butterflies.
They are brief and beautiful.
The Siren song is not unfamiliar to me.
It is just beyond a horizon
That propels my search for dreams.

I have lived many loves and heartbreaks.
I know of beauty, of that first illusion
Fundamental to what beats.
I know about that wild and necessary force of the species in heat.
It is a mandate of the living
Like the passion that pulses and enlivens the senses
And shrouds us in the now that becomes eternal.

But the time advances, and goodbyes are made with memories--
Long and deep like rivers.
We are alive! Everything ends and it is redeeming.
We are like a stream, and love is a channel
To the salt of the seas to the forces that blow towards the shore
To the ample ocean that moves us,
And to the gift of life that is a love that does not end.

I have lived the pain and the resurgence of hope.
I rearrange looks and words,
The light and the melody,
The flap of wings, the flow of water,
And the seed.

Everything stays in what's beautiful and necessary.
Everything remains intact in light.
Although the flower itself may not be what adorns a vase
Nor the same wave dampens the shore,
Not even the song of the same bird in space.

The days are so long and so beautiful.
The chest is so spacious, so intense and profound.
The warm hug, the kisses, the memories,
And the everyday chores and dreams.

At my age, I have added Passion,
Great loves, indelible,
Immense, and eternal.
Generations carry our banner,
Companions who still see the hidden fire of the lips
And the intense look of the search for the distant horizon.

At my age, I understand
Love does not end.
It becomes spacious.

by Carmen E. Arroyo
Translated by Edna Iris Garcia

## NEW AUTUMN LOVE

It silhouettes my fuller curves,
irons wrinkles into dunes,
softens parched lips,

nudges me into dancing
on the tips of ten toes
each time I ripple into love.

It threads gold up my spine,
silver-streaking me
from belly to brain.

Every touch offering
opalescence to the wind
beneath full moons,

every sigh, a quiet water flow
into gently gathering rivers,

the undercurves of my feet
telling this new story.

A deepening inner me, wiser,
speaking a new language.

My head,
after decades,
cobweb lace light.

by Claire Joysmth

**35th Anniversary**

This skin of road too glistening to
take my eyes off from the faint white line,
offers me more than I can handle,
the bend, a sleeping lover's knee,
hints that I need to slow down,
can kick back if I move too fast.

My car still skids, just inches near the rough edge.
Will I never learn? I always overcompensate for everything.
Finally, I've eased around the tree-lined pavement
slip-sliding me to my destination,
made it over the road's steel-lined gratings
and past the meadow, crisp with fingers of ice.

I'm following my husband's telephone directions,
but sometimes our language speeds past each other.
Our voice-over-voice must reach past the hazards
to find the way, meet halfway along this marriage
we travel through, interpret the signs,
those easily missed messages, through each season.

I do arrive, as does he, here at our anniversary getaway,
where directions are no longer the issue,
where the beach spreads safely.
Not needing words, we walk
solidly unswerving.

by Cynthia Pratt

## House of Silence

[i] live in a house of silent noises—
noises that are deafening in their voluminous hollowness,
noises that whisper screams of emptiness
that nag and prod and poke in the side of my dissolving comfort
while the silent clock strikes chords of toiling vacancies
where love used to live.
Silence screams like sirens on a shady Saturday night.
There is a wall of thick silence smoldering like smog between us
layering our lives like the tower of power horns filling the spaces
of whom we used to be. . ..

[i] live in a house of silence. . ..

Small breaths taken like calculating thoughts
evaporate quickly before the other can recognize the emotion.
My chest heaves under the weight of unused words.
The bed in the other room squeaks
with subtle movements of restless nights.
Each can hear the mind of the other clanging—
changing, contemplating, then finally disregarding the notion
of breaking the wrought-iron nothingness of no words.
In the beginning, there was the silence. And now, it raises its dragon head
and smothers us in the smoke of its web of soundlessness.

[i] live in a house of silence...

...an atmosphere filled with old words that hover like ancient ruins,
words that linger like worn pictures speaking a thousand lost thoughts
where mouths remain muted by Egos determined to reign
even if for the crown of an impotent victory...
Our castrated tongues plucked
by the furiously fierce fingers of human haughtiness...

[i] live in a house of silence...

where no one responds to my protest of wordlessness,
and my muted declarations fall on unlistening ears
filled to capacity with cotton balls of stillness that weigh heavy
blocking the reception of poisonous phonemes.

[i] live in a house of silence...

where the opening door squeals like piercing pleas for redemption,
and water drops bluntly into the bottom of empty cups,
shattering silence's stream of sterile consciousness.
With the hands of my heart, [i] push against the transparent but heavy hush;
but to no avail for the steel beams of silence are planted purposefully into the
cemented foundation of needing desperately to be right

more than needing to be loved...
In the middle of sound cessation, the phone rings
like the trumpet on the last day, but neither of us answers,
condemning our relationship to the damnation of improper quiet.
The sound of passing cars rudely breaks the flow of reticence,
but like interrupted water, silence slowly wavers and smooths
once again into its constant glass-like still ...

[i] live in a house of silence...

Our vocabulary is desolate as the field of our relationship
becomes weeded with an awed silence of insignificant murmurs.
We have built a temple of soundless babble to the gods of obstinacy—
not even Eshu has the power to raise the dead of our deceased lexicon.
For we have become unable to signify with the coconuts of our souls
and barren brown branches show a fleeting fall into the winter of dyslexia
from pith to bark fifty rings fading into the rotting rhetoric.

[i] live in the house of silence with my mate and our wedded worthlessness.

by C. Liegh McInnis

**Love's Equation**
**(for Michael)**

Hope the phone bill isn't too high.
All he did last week was call
me from out of town.
Today he finally came home with
three red roses, so I made him
twelve blueberry muffins.
For hours we kissed under moonlight
touching his mouth with my tongue,
that electric tongue.
I put his two suitcases away,
telling him to please be careful
with my clean floor.
Maybe one million times
I've told that man not to
make such as mess!
After twenty years, who's counting?

by Joan McNerney

**To A Lady**

It's nice beyond a certain stage

(merely a synonym for age)

to leave behind the vexing task

of falling, thrice a day, in love

often by the broadest light, thereof;

and, hormone-driven, bear Love's cross—

charming, awfully, the way

secretions frack our mortal clay

such as a shower cannot remedy—

ardor writ with future inanition;

abandoned more in practice than in theory,

now; then, I never minded, really—

a "pay the present, shirk

the future" policy retired,

I recall one fact:

this Love's a lot of *work*.

by Robert Dickerson

**Late-life Love**

Surely my passion, when I was younger
was just a function of heat and hunger.
What did I know then but lust and fire,
nothing of warmth and sweet desire?

Time was caught up in sex and its surges,
pressing pulses, and desperate urges.
I thought affection was ardor only
not for the luckless, not for the lonely.

Convinced that I must respond in haste
since lovers had so little time to waste,
I thought that age would make us colder,
but fires are banked as one grows older.

So, enjoy the fervor, the early thrill,
but it gets better. Oh, it will. It will.

by Kathy Lundy Derengowski

**Profound Love**

Love as elusive as time,
As profound as God,
As absolute as death,
I long for you.
Even though life stole my youth and beauty,
I welcome you with abandonment.

Love as elusive as time,
As profound as God,
As absolute as death,
It matters not that my body is tired.
My flesh, wrinkled from years of toil,
Still wants passion's warmth.

Love as elusive as time,
As profound as God,
As absolute as death,
Find me now and see me as I am.
Let your ardor lift me higher
And fill me before the coming of dusk.

by Edna Garcia

**Archived**

Short-term memory loss is similar
to watching TV commercials.
The memories ask for my attention,
only to lose it by
the next round of remembrances.
Other times that loss of short-term memories
reminds me of movie trailers.
Although the memories are loud
and lavishly bright with self-importance,
in the end, they leave no inerasable image.
Sometimes short-term memories
can appear like billboards
through an express train window,
flashing briefly as the locomotive
moves to the next station.
At this station of my mature life,
I am content just having a long-term
memory of once loving you.

by Bob McNeil

# GRIZZLED GRACE

Late as always,
we lie down tired,
do nightly gymnastics of twists—
straighten pajama legs, tug at sleeves,
wrestle blankets, rumple around,

punch pillows—work their loft
to take weight off arthritic elbows,
and injured shoulders.
This gawky jerk-and-flop,
a new dance we do each night.

At last, pantlegs and armholes aligned,
your good ear muzzled in fiberfill,
body cupped behind my own like a comma
to shush cold breath of night and pause
this long day's rumpus,
you snake your free arm over my ribs
and hook me close so I won't slip away.

I hope old Sandman comes along
before I need to grope through the dark
to the john, or turn my body over—
a slow lift-and-shift
that draws protest from a bad-tempered hip.

This is our moment of bliss—
this wink of grizzled grace before sleep.
Nestled in place,
we lie here awake
to the tune of each other's whistled breathing
this last, best minute of the day.

by Susan McMillan

**The Old Lovers**

Tonight, as my arthritic ankle nestles
into the sunken small of your bad back,
my crooked finger runs along the slack-
line of your gray jaw.  Sclerotic vessels
hamper blood to muscles cramped like pretzels.
Beneath my head, I hear the creak and crack
of your sore shoulder.  My sacroiliac
complains in silence as joy and comfort wrestle.

It does not matter.  Others might eulogize
Romeo and Juliet, but Shakespeare
never gave them time to realize
the length and depth of secrets we hold dear.
You kiss the crow's feet etched around my eyes.
I whisper words of love in your deaf ear.

by Kit Rohrbach

**The Sum of Maturity's Rhythm**

Once the brilliantly babyish bliss
Of your life fades from each iris,
Once the percussionist behind your chest
Has no vitality for life's song to invest,
Once your libido is as fickle as traffic,
Unsure whether it will be kinetic or lethargic,
You continue living to see
How much damage Time's demolition crew
Will do to the building housing you.
Hopefully, regardless of the wreckage,
Someone will remain with you in a
Friendship or marriage.
Then, every so often,
Life and love can seem
Comparable to silver or gold.
Companionship is a valued gem
When becoming old.

by Bob McNeil

# Just Hold Me

"Sex doesn't disappear, it just changes forms." — Erica Jong

**waiting for magic**

much more than before
slowest grayest oldest
waiting for magic
aging in a crowd

slowest grayest oldest
starved for affection
aging in a crowd
poor man pays for lust

starved for affection
never could persuade
poor man pays for lust
lap dance twenty bucks

never could persuade
women I desire fade
lap dance twenty bucks
I pay the price

women I desire fade
much more than before
I pay the price
waiting for magic

by Fred Simpson

**Untitled**

when an old man dreams of sex
he dreams of his first wife
the young one
eager
moist lips, soft cheeks
necking on her parents' doorstep
knocking her up in his sister's bedroom
when he was just a boy
when an old man dreams of sex
he dreams of his second wife
the smart one
who knew what she wanted and how to get it
quid pro quo
naked in the forest
willing to be taken
always on top
Odysseus, it has been said
did hew his sumptuous wedding bed
with a single mighty stroke
from the heart of a living oak
when an old man dreams of sex
he dreams of his third wife
the bitter one
counting the minutes
head to the side
turning her back
arm's distance
taking care of business
waiting for it to be over
when an old man dreams of sex
he dreams of his last wife
the silent one
withdrawn
eyes closed
rigid
unresponsive
insensate
lying in the cold, cold ground
Penelope, the constant wife
spent the best part of her life
wrestling with the surly crowd
weaving her husband's funeral shroud

by E. Penniman James

**Just hold me**

Senior sex is not always an estuary.
Sometimes a rivulet will do.
Just hold me.  Just hold me.

Passion doesn't have to hit a middle c's high,
Like a soprano in an opera.
Often soft low tones soothe and satisfy.

Affection is not celluloid excitement.
Faking interest is better left on the screen.
Honest love is an awardable achievement.

Just hold me.  Just hold me.

by Jean Parrish

**Dirty Old Lady**

Hello there, young man,
younger than my son.
You're short and not pretty.
My womanly intuition
tells me you're lonely.
In your work, you meet only
seniors like me.

What if I assured you
you're smart and witty,
adorable even,
and soon someone
will surely love you?

What if I told you,
(careful not to touch your arm,)
that when I was young,
it could have been me?

by Leslie Mills

# Your body deserts you
"Let mortal man keep to his own Mortality, and not expect too much."
--Euripides

**Your Body Deserts You**

Your body deserts you

no matter the diet,

the plan, treadmills,

and nutritionists,

massages, and

acupuncture,

your body deserts you,

your sagging skin

tells you, so

and only a quiet soul

can lie in peace

and let it go.

We are morphing creations:

tender babies rocked in a crib,

know-it-all adolescents

hanging at a mall,

harried first jobbers

out to please the boss,

diligent parents with

a newborn to feed,

middle-aged parents with

a college bill to pay,

retirees in Florida

with nothing much to do,

hoping that the kids

will visit soon.

Then your body deserts you

and despite the morphine drip,

the neurologists, the serologists,

the EEGs and the EKGs

and the prayers from your alma mater,

it doesn't matter,

your body deserts you,

and only a quiet soul

will lie in peace

and let it go.

by Edward Thomas Dillon

**Rearview Mirror**

In my rearview mirror
on this fatal journey, objects
are closer than they appear:
the needle the nurse preps
for your Lupron injection,
your gray-cloaked, shuffling fatigue,
your angry sunrises.

In my rearview mirror, passenger-side
as I join you for the fatal ride,
time seems quicker
between PSA test counts,
bad news, good news, no news
days, a blur of Medicare forms, oncology
records, vials of blood-red impatience.

In my rearview mirror, as I navigate
for us this fatal itinerary,
distances grow shorter
from abetting testosterone to blazing
cancer cells, from the clinical heart
to cynical brain, from
hope to fear.

by Karla Linn Merrifield

**The Caretaker**

Inside Hollybrook House on its suburban half-acre,
I sit at my desk, scouring photo files of a trek
or two up the Amazon, another down the Nile. I retrace
our pathways on an African safari, the Antarctic expedition—the arc
of the planet, our seven oceans and ten thousand islands—the art
of connubial love to the ends of the earth, then—whoosh!—home to the terra
firma of a hospital bed, you facing sunny side, our front yard, your gingko tree,
as I watch you fading—so swift— glimpses of you now rare.
I know full well from many expert sources: dementia leaves no trace.
Too soon, too soon, my husband, you are. . ..

by Karla Linn Merrifield

# Me and my burden of bones

"Death is like a robe everyone has to wear." – an African Proverb

**Embraceable You**

I have run away from you for sixty-eight

years, running as fast as I could to

every doctor's appointment: the lung guy,

the skin woman, the nose dude who took

away my sense of smell, but at least

I could breathe.

Like a sprinter on a mission, I

passed the baton to these healers

not looking for immortality but a

reasonably long lifespan having passed

so many too soon:

Paul, 16, run over on his bike.

Billy, 18, suffered from leukemia.

Shelly, 27, hung herself in a closet.

Dwayne, 20, shot in Vietnam.

Franco, 17, wasn't wearing his seatbelt.

The Twins, 17, weren't wearing their seatbelts

either, and the guy, 45, with the kids who

fell asleep on his way home from work.

There aren't enough pages to list

all the dead, and if you reach the

age of about 20, they begin to accumulate

like Judy, 23, who rolled over her VW bug on

her way home from the restaurant and looked

like she was sleeping in her coffin.

The list just gets longer, but no less

painful through your thirties and forties

and fifties and now

I'm my parents' age,

and I remember them

staring at each other as they returned

from the latest funeral mass or kneeled by

a coffin of their aunt, uncle, cousin or friend

who died too soon. I remember their

pallid faces when they returned from

cousin Peter's wake.

Cousin Peter, 23, drove his motorcycle into a truck.

Cousin Peter, my mother said, looked just like you.

They surround us, the dead,

in dusty marble mausoleums,

under acres of stone,

in tiny boxes placed on mantles,

their ashes waiting to

be scattered to an unsuspecting wind.

Our imagination toils for it all,

an explanation by the living for the dead,

those resurrected zombies who want

to eat your brain, tear you apart

and dive into your liver

Or, is it the resurrected soul that

travels through the tunnel of light

to Godland: no pain, no bills,

eternal bliss and salvation, no

worrying about eating people's parts

or dodging the next mass murderer?

Of course, there's the alternative,

where the final sum of your earthly

transgressions sends you to the

Badlands where Satan makes

mincemeat of your soul and dines

on your spleen every night for eternity.

You'd see a lot of your friends there,

and they would look just as miserable as you.

My Dad thought he'd go to Godland,

and he refused to get a hip replacement

because he wanted to have all his

original parts when he was resurrected,

body intact, brand new,

for being a good Catholic.

My Dad, 79, suffered for five years with Parkinson's.

I dwell in an earthly firmament

where I am married to the

angel of my dreams, where my

little old dog thinks she's a puppy,

where my friends check in on me, and

I call them and let them know they

are loved, where music fills my days,

and I build joy with my hammer.

This morning I was out kayaking

with some friends on a river, and

the kayak flipped, and I had trouble

righting myself. For about a second,

I was nervous, so I calmed myself by

floating on my back, and my

friends righted the kayak to

complete the paddle on the Mattapoisett River

which is why I get to write this last line:

Eddie, 68, loving his beloved,

still living in Heaven.

by Edward Thomas Dillon

**Her Candle**

So many candles I've never burned:
a marriage candle,
two first communion candles for my kids,
a bicentennial candle,
a millennium candle,
So many candles I've never burned.

Her candle I've burned for over twenty years,
not every day, but most every day.
A memory of what once was,
of what we had,
me and her.
Her candle,
originally voluptuously large,
beautifully ornate,
burning bright hot and fast.
We were young then.

Gradually her candle grew old,
became hollow,
most of the outside still holding fast,
dusty with age,
the wick long lost,
in darkness temporarily filled
with a tea light candle.
Certain songs, movies, or moods
seem to rekindle the freshness,
remind me of when her candle was new.
In the light of day, reality blazes,
her candle, actually an empty shell,
so hard to visualize as it once was,
as in last night's memory.

Beginning to wonder,
continuing to wonder,
if, after all this time,
I shouldn't just throw it out.
This foolish vigil,
senseless old man,
end this memorial,
this ritual, and move on.

But, as the room grows dark,
the many candles I've never burned
remain so.
A new tea light candle
and she is back,
we, me and her,

her candle
and my thoughts
of twenty years ago.

by Carl Palmer

## Me and My Burden of Bones

With my eye on the end of the road,
my ear to the ground,
my mouth speaking into the wind,
I go forward as all must.
A burden of bones
weighs heavy on my back.
My clothes are simple,
a mere sack with nothing inside.
The road is winding and rocky.
I know not how it will end,
but we all meet the same destination
in the end.
A simple affair,
a grave, whether in the ground
or in the sea, it all comes out the same.
We are made of dust.
From dust we come
to dust we go.
I move my burden of bones
uneasily upon my shoulder
and head on.
I am on my way.

by Will Mayo

**Between The Pages Of A Life**

What more is there to life?
A doing, a dying,
something lost between,
Words cannot encompass it all,
Nor can prayers.
Lovers pause hand in hand
to look at a sunset,
thinking it will last forever.
It never does.
But between the love lost and the love gained,
there is something of peace.
Herons stand in the seawater,
their beaks full of fish.
Damn, isn't it lovely just the same?

by Will Mayo

## Notes on the Poets

**Carmen E. Arroyo** was born in Puerto Rico. She is a former Special Education and ESL educator. Carmen attained a BA in Psychology from The University of Puerto Rico. At present, she is retired and enjoys making sculptures and taking art classes. Above all else, Carmen considers her daughter to be the greatest gift in life.

**Silvia Blumenfeld** is a creative arts therapist who worked with differently-abled people in long-term care and psychiatric settings. She currently co-teaches a writing and storytelling class at Lehman College (CUNY). She's a graduate of Barnard College and received her Master of Science at Lehman. Furthermore, she's an artist, writer, mother, and grandmother who lives and works in the Bronx.

**Kathy Lundy Derengowski** is a native of San Diego county. She is an active member and co-facilitator of the Lake San Marcos Writer's Workshop. Her work has appeared in the *San Diego Poetry Annual, Summation, the ekphrasis anthology of the Escondido Arts Partnership, California Quarterly, Silver Birch Press, Autumn Sky Daily, Turtle Light Press* and the *Journal of Modern Poetry*. Besides being a guest blogger on Trish Hopkinson's Selfish Poet site, she won awards from the California State Poetry Society.

**Robert Dickerson** has published five collections of poetry. A sixth entitled *Differences* is due out soon. His work has been awarded in the WB Yeats poetry competition and has appeared in many anthologies and journals. He nods to the canon and is a self-described formalist. Furthermore, he thanks the editor for inclusion in this anthology.

**Edward Thomas Dillon** wrote: "I am a professional musician who has performed in the Irish music world for many decades, most notably with the Clancy Brothers in the 1990's. My current projects include YouTube animations and a new CD to be released in late winter. Aside from having written over 500 songs, my writing projects include two novels, an autobiography and a musical as well as a collection of several hundred poems."

**Edna Iris Garcia** was born in Humacao, Puerto Rico. She received a BA and Master's Degree in Bilingual Education. Also, Edna was the first Latina in the Connecticut General Assembly. For over forty years, she served her community with notable distinction. As a result, she received numerous awards for her effort to better the city and state. At present, she is on the precipice of finishing a semi-autobiographical novel.

**Linda Imbler** has five published poetry collections and one hybrid e-book of short fiction and poetry. She is a Kansas-based Pushcart Prize and Best of the Net Nominee. More information about her can be found at lindaspoetryblog.blogspot.com.

**E. Penniman James** (67) lives and writes poetry in Brooklyn. He reads frequently at spoken word events and jazz jam sessions in NYC. His poem, "they came to watch him bleed," appears in Great Weather for Media's 2018 anthology Birds Fall Silent in the Mechanical Sea.

**Claire Joysmth** has published bilingual poetry and memoir, critical and creative essays, as well as translations throughout the Americas and Europe. Recently retired as Professor, she lives in Yucatán, Mexico **(http://clairejoysmith.blogspot.com).**

**John Maney** is a published poet, freelance writer, workshop leader, photographer, and Publisher of the "Finding Your Voice Newsletter."

**Will Mayo**'s books include *Hoodoo Voodoo And Other Strange Stories Of Life* and *Dreams Of Mongolia And Other Stories* and *Poems From One Man's Mind*, which are available on Amazon. He takes heart in his hometown of eccentrics and wanderers among its clustered spires and with the good of heart everywhere.

**C. Liegh McInnis** is a poet, short story writer, author of eight books, former editor of Black Magnolias Literary Journal, and an English instructor at Jackson State University. He is also a former First Runner-Up of the Amiri Baraka/Sonia Sanchez Poetry Award sponsored by North Carolina State A&T.

**Susan McMillan** is a Minnesota poet who lives with her husband of 42 years on wooded acreage. She spends her free time tramping around in the woods or canoeing the beautiful lakes of the Boundary Waters. She strives to promote poetry and create opportunities for poets in her community and currently serves the city of Rochester as the Poet Laureate.

**Bob McNeil**, writer, editor, and spoken word artist, is the author of *Verses of Realness*. Hal Sirowitz, a Queens Poet Laureate, called the book "A fantastic trip through the mind of a poet who doesn't flinch at the truth." Among Bob's recent accomplishments, he found working on *Lyrics of Mature Hearts* to be a humbling experience because of the anthology's talented contributors.

**Joan McNerney**'s poetry has been included in numerous literary magazines such as *Seven Circle Press*, *Dinner with the Muse*, *Poet Warriors*, *Blueline*, and *Halcyon Days*. Four Bright Hills Press Anthologies, several *Poppy Road Review* journals, and numerous *Kind of A Hurricane Press* publications have accepted her work. Her latest title, *The Muse In Miniature*, is available on Amazon, and she has four Best of the Net nominations.

**Karla Linn Merrifield** has 14 books to her credit. Following her 2018 *Psyche's Scroll* (Poetry Box Select) is the newly released full-length book *Athabaskan Fractal: Poems of the Far North* from Cirque Press. She is currently at work on a poetry collection, *My Body the Guitar*, inspired by famous guitarists and their guitars; the book is slated to be published in December 2021 by Before Your Quiet Eyes Publications Holograph Series (Rochester, NY).

**Kevin Miller** taught in the public schools of Washington State for thirty-nine years. His fourth collection *Vanish* won the Wandering Aengus Publication Prize in 2019.

**Leslie Mills** is a former music teacher. She divides her year between New York City and Arisaig, Nova Scotia, a fishing village, where she gardens.

**Carl "Papa" Palmer** of Old Mill Road in Ridgeway, Virginia, lives in University Place, Washington. He is retired from the military and Federal Aviation Administration (FAA), enjoying life as "Papa" to his grand descendants and being a Franciscan Hospice volunteer. Carl is a Pushcart Prize, Best of the Net, and Micro Award nominee.

Going as far back as grammar school, **Jean Parrish** always adored literature, specifically poetry. Even now, during her fifties, her interest has not waned. Although Jean compulsively writes, she never pursued her passion on a professional basis. She composed poems for a single purpose—therapy. Finally, at the behest of a friend, she amassed enough courage to submit some of her work to this anthology.

Influenced by James Baldwin, Rome Neal, Sonia Sanchez, and Amiri Baraka, **Lydia Elizabeth Percy** is an American poet from Queens, New York. She received the 1987 Literary Achievement Award and the Ntozake Shange Poets Award. Lydia is a member of NWU/UAW, Local 1981/AFL-CIO. Moreover, she is the author of *Pussy Toes*.

**Cynthia Pratt** is a founding member of the Olympia Poetry Network's board, which has been in existence for 30 years. Her poems appeared in WPA's anthology, *Tattoos on Cedar* (2006), *Crab Creek Review*, *Steelhead Special*, *Raven Chronicles*, *Bellingham Review*, *Godiva Speaks*, and other publications and is the author of *Celestial Drift*. She is the Deputy Mayor of the City of Lacey.

**Kit Rohrbach** lives, writes, and herds cats in southeast Minnesota.

**Fred Simpson** is a poet, percussionist, playwright, and songwriter. His poems appear in several publications, including *Riverside Poets Anthology* (vols. 13-18), *Dinner with the Muse* (vols. 2&3), *Mobius*, *Poetry Magazine*, the 29th & 30th editions, *Culvert Chronicles*, and *Estrellas en el Fuego*. Fred enjoys drumming. His eclectic percussion skills are evident when he performs with Gemini Journey as well as fronting a jazz trio. His book, *Just Another Sunrise, Poems to the Sun*, is available at Amazon.com and from the author at simpsonfnyc@gmail.com.

**James Walton** was a librarian, a farm laborer, and mostly a public sector union official. He appears in many anthologies, journals, and newspapers. His poetry collections include *The Leviathan's Apprentice*, *Walking Through Fences*, *Unstill Mosaics*, and *Abandoned Soliloquies*. He is now old enough to be almost invisible.

**Jonathan Yungkans** is a Los Angeles-based writer and photographer with an MFA in poetry from California State University, Long Beach. His work has appeared in *San Pedro River Review*, *Synkroniciti*, *West Texas Literary Review*, and other publications. He has written two poetry chapbooks; the second of these, *Beyond a Glazed Shimmer*, won the 2019 Clockwise Chapbook Award and is slated for release by Tebor Bach Publishing in 2020.

## About the Publisher

**Gordon P. Bois** was born on November 9, 1969, in Espanola, Ontario, Canada. For many years, he wrote poetry, prose, experimental texts, and inspirational quotes. He published several collections of poetry and quotes.

*Lyrics of Mature Hearts* is his first publication that showcases other poets, who, like himself, passionately embrace the written word.

CPSIA information can be obtained
at www.ICGtesting.com
Printed in the USA
LVHW042051030520
654928LV00005B/1414

9 781708 365356